W9-ANZ-625

# OUR ENDANGERED EARTH

# DAVID COOK
# BIRDS

## CONTENTS

CROWN PUBLISHERS INC. NEW YORK

The white stork is a victim of industrialization in northern Europe. It used to come each spring from Africa to nest on buildings in the towns and villages. Here it was welcome, an omen of good luck. Cooler summers combined with pollution to destroy it. Now white storks are very rare in many areas, and extinct in others.

**Successful birds**
House sparrows, rock doves and barn swallows nest on buildings. European starlings seek the warm cities to roost at night.

house sparrow

European starling

rock dove

# Birds and people

Whether you live in the town or the country, birds are a familiar everyday sight. But the birds you see around you are nearly always limited to a few of the most common types (or species), such as sparrows and blackbirds, pigeons and gulls, and so on.

This is because the birds that have survived in the greatest numbers are the ones which have adapted best to the way humans have changed the world.

Among these are town pigeons, which find buildings a good substitute for the cliffs they used to inhabit. Swifts, swallows and martins, once cave and cliff-dwellers, now settle successfully in towns. Gulls and crows thrive on the scraps and waste food found around human habitation.

But not all birds are so lucky or so adaptable, and many species have been made extinct, or are in danger.

Birds have adapted to their natural surroundings over millions of years, and some of them have been unable to cope with the changes brought about by people. As the human population has grown, wild land has been cultivated and farmed, forests cut down and marshes drained to grow crops and rear livestock. All this has deprived birds of their natural habitat.

There are still 8,650 species of birds in the world today, but about 80 species have become extinct in the last three hundred years. Many more are threatened.

Most birds that died out in the past were killed as an accidental result of our attempt to tame nature, in ignorance of the harm this was doing to wild birds. But today we are more aware of their problems, and of the need to protect them and give all the remaining species a chance to survive.

European kestrels hunt along roadsides and on vacant land. Wood-pigeons, red-winged blackbirds and quelea finches feed on our crops.

barn swallow

red-winged blackbird

wood pigeon

European kestrel

quelea finch
Southern Africa

# Evolution and extinction

Birds are descended from reptiles. Scales were replaced by feathers, cold blood by warm blood, and birds emerged as a completely distinct animal from their reptilian ancestors.

This process of transformation is called evolution. Living things gradually change, giving rise to new forms of life which can survive better in a world that is itself perpetually changing.

Birds evolved about 160 million years ago, and the species that survive today are those which adapted successfully to their changing surroundings during all those millions of years.

Scientists have divided all birds into

hermosiornis

Hermosiornis was one of a group of huge flesh-eating ground birds which lived in South America millions of years ago. These became extinct quite naturally. They could not compete with meat-eating mammals which came down from North America.

The 3.3 feet-long seriema is the only descendant of the giant seriema. It is a very poor flier, and is often kept with chickens. This is because it eats snakes and other vermin. It is a very good watch-dog, screaming at strangers as they approach.

seriema

twenty-seven groups (or orders) of birds related to each other. The most adaptable, and therefore the most successful order is that of perching birds, which range from ravens to tiny wrens, and which make up two-thirds of all bird species.

Other orders have been less successful: since birds first evolved it is thought that at least half a million species have become extinct. The order which includes cranes thrived when more of the world was swampland. But swamps have been shrinking naturally for millions of years, and many species within that order are now extinct. More recently, many birds have become extinct, or are threatened with extinction, because humans have been tampering with the natural environment.

In the last few hundred years, people have taken over most of the world's land, clearing forests, draining marshes, farming, and building cities. The effect of man-made change is very different from that of natural change. Natural change is a slow process which gives birds time to adapt or evolve into better-equipped life forms. But the changes people make are so sudden that birds have no time to adapt, and nowhere to go once their habitat has been destroyed.

Unless we take action now, the less adaptable species will die out, and the great variety of bird life will be lost.

The panel shows some Hawaiian birds which have become extinct because of the changes made to their habitat in recent years.

The Carolina parakeet was common until settlers came to North America. It was thought to harm fruit trees, and so was killed.

7

# Island birds

Island birds are more vulnerable than birds that live on the great land masses. Their environment has made them less adaptable, and also less able to defend themselves against their enemies.

The first island birds arrived by chance, probably blown there on the wind. In time, whole colonies grew up, completely isolated from the rest of the world. Some of the islands they inhabited were formed by volcanic action, and others, like New Zealand, were cut off from the mainlands before the rise of mammals. This meant that for millions of years island birds lived in ideal surroundings. No other animals competed with them for food, and no animals hunted them. The birds lost all fear. They didn't need to conceal their nests. And some even lost their ability to fly because they had no enemies.

The arrival of the early explorers was disastrous for these innocent birds, which were suddenly exposed to dangers they had never met before. Many of them, including the dodo, were slaughtered for food. More recently, during the Second World War (1939–45), the flightless Wake Island rail was exterminated to provide food for a starving garrison of soldiers.

An even greater threat to the birds was the introduction of other animals to their islands. Rats infested the early ships and came ashore to eat eggs, fledglings and even adult birds of many species. On Captain

**The fate of the dodo**

When explorers first found the Mascarene Islands in the Indian Ocean, they discovered the dodo.

Larger than a turkey, tame and flightless, it was killed to provide fresh meat for visiting sailors.

But many survived inland. These were exterminated by pigs and monkeys which settlers had brought.

These animals preyed on both the eggs and the fledglings of the survivors. By 1680 the dodo was extinct.

Cook's famous voyages of discovery between 1769–78 seven new species were found on various islands, all of which had died out by the time the ships returned.

When humans began to settle on the larger islands, they brought domestic animals with them. Many birds were then killed by cats, dogs, and even pigs.

Nine-tenths of all birds recorded as being extinct were from islands. Even today, many of our most endangered birds are island-dwellers. Rats and other introduced animals still live on the islands. Farming methods have changed the land, the livestock has eaten much of the natural vegetation. The world to which the birds had adapted no longer exists.

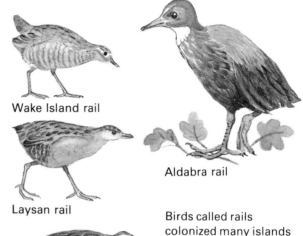

Wake Island rail

Laysan rail

Aldabra rail

Macquarie Island rail

Birds called rails colonized many islands in the Indian and Pacific Oceans. Many evolved to be flightless. At least 15 species are now extinct. Of those shown, only the Aldabra rail still survives.

The giant New Zealand moas, which could grow 13.2 feet tall, was hunted to extinction by the Maoris who settled there 600 years ago.

The kiwi (above) of New Zealand is protected by the country and is its national emblem. The tahaké is a flightless bird which was thought extinct. But a colony was found in 1948 in a remote part of South Island, and still thrives.

9

# Introduced birds

People have changed the distribution of birds in the world by introducing foreign species into new areas. This can sometimes happen accidentally when birds escape from zoos or aviaries and then reproduce in the wild. But many introductions have been intentional. For example, pheasants and partridges have been introduced into many countries all over the world to provide sport for hunters. These game birds do not present a threat to the existing native birds, but many other introduced birds do. If alien birds become established, native birds often have to compete with them for survival, and suffer as a result.

In New Zealand, for instance, settlers who were nostalgic for the sights and sounds of home introduced European birds. There are now thirteen species there,

Barn owls were brought to the Seychelles Islands in the Indian Ocean, to combat a plague of rats. They are one reason why the Seychelles kestrel is endangered. The owls compete for food.

**Starlings**
European starlings were introduced to New York in 1890. The map shows how quickly they spread across America. Now millions live here. They are often a pest on a scale unknown in Europe, where predators and other competing birds combine to keep the population in check.

1955
1945
1925
1890

— spread of starlings

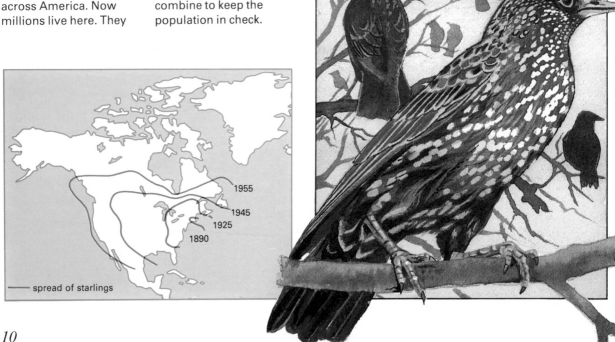

including blackbirds, thrushes, starlings, sparrows and larks. These European birds were already adapted to living on farmland and near people. As more land was cultivated they increased in number. But the native New Zealand birds had no chance to adapt and could not compete with the newcomers. Now they are confined to ever-shrinking areas of unspoiled land.

Alien birds can also bring diseases against which the native birds have no resistance. The American wild turkey, for instance, nearly became extinct because of fowl sickness spread from domestic chickens.

Mindful of these hazards to native birds, some countries have laws to prevent the introduction of alien species. But as long as people keep aviaries, there is always a risk of escape.

Red-whiskered bulbuls from China are a common aviary bird. Some escaped from aviaries. Now they thrive in the United States and Australia.

Starlings roost in the warmth of cities in the winter. They compete with native birds for food, leaving less for the latter to eat.

Starlings nest in holes and drive away other birds seeking nesting holes.

# Hunting for profit

Commercial shooting and trapping accounted for many bird casualties in the past. When the early settlers colonized North America there was an abundance of wild birds, which were a cheap source of food for the growing human population.

Huge flocks of wild ducks were killed. The Eskimo curlew, which migrated between the Americas in their millions, was so ruthlessly hunted that it is doubtful whether any survive at all today. The passenger pigeon, once the most common bird in North America, was hunted to extinction. The last one died in a zoo.

Other species suffered because of the feather trade. A huge population of great auks, a flightless penguin-like bird, lived on Funk Island off Newfoundland until the 1790s. Then a demand for their feathers to make pillows and mattresses led to their slaughter, and they were extinct by 1844. Early this century, the fashion for wearing ornamental feathers resulted in the slaughter of many plumed birds. Some waders, such as the Chinese egret, never recovered and are still extremely rare.

Today, the most widespread and commercially profitable trade in birds is in live birds for zoos, aviaries and pet shops. Parrots, a favorite among bird pets,

The snowy egret was nearly exterminated in North America by feather hunters. Now it is protected.

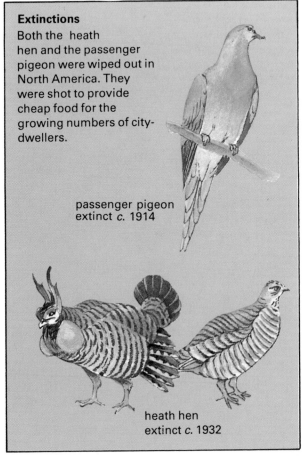

**Extinctions**
Both the heath hen and the passenger pigeon were wiped out in North America. They were shot to provide cheap food for the growing numbers of city-dwellers.

passenger pigeon extinct c. 1914

heath hen extinct c. 1932

belong to one of the groups under the greatest pressure. The rarer species are in particular demand because they fetch higher prices.

Unfortunately, many birds caught for the pet trade are killed or injured as they are captured, and many more die during transportation. Few of those captured birds which do survive have a chance to breed.

Of course, bird catching alone will not destroy a whole species, but it is an added threat to birds which are already endangered. Consequently, a world-wide effort is being made to control the trade and to confine it to birds which are not rare.

scarlet macaws

The South American macaw is one of the species sought by the pet trade. If too many are taken it could become endangered.

# Hunting for pleasure

The shooting of birds is a world-wide sport, and in countries where hunting is strictly regulated the hunted species are not endangered. Sometimes they can even prosper because although many of them are killed, many more are reared artificially. A lot of game birds have been introduced into new areas where they can thrive and multiply.

At one time the capercaillie was hunted to extinction in Scotland. But it has now been re-introduced and is no longer a threatened species there. Similarly, the wild turkey, which once neared extinction in North America, has been re-introduced into many places where it previously lived.

In some cases, however, hunting can do great damage. Hunting for ducks and geese is a popular pursuit. These are mostly migratory birds and are truly wild. Many are already threatened because their natural habitat, the wetlands, are being drained, and their numbers are falling. Hunting can expose them to more risk, however carefully the sport is controlled.

In countries where hunting is not regulated, the shooting of birds can have serious consequences. The Great Indian bustard living on the Indian plains is a victim of uncontrolled hunting and poaching. In common with bustards all over the world, they also face the problem of a shrinking natural habitat because of land being taken over for cultivation. Now the Indian bustard is very rare, and less than a thousand remain. Unlike many game birds they breed very slowly, and will not do so at all in captivity, so there is little hope of re-introducing them if the native population dies out in the wild.

Common game birds, such as the ordinary ring-necked pheasant, are hardy enough to survive, and have been successfully introduced all over the world. But ornamental pheasants, most of which originally came from the Orient, have become extremely rare, due to the destruction of their habitat, combined with uncontrolled hunting. However, there is hope of saving these birds because they are not only prolific breeders, but they also thrive in captivity. Now, many are bred in zoos and aviaries so that stocks of them can be maintained. Ideally, they will one day be returned to their true homes.

These game birds owe their survival to the help and protection offered by sportsmen.

capercaillie

ring-necked pheasant

wild turkey

Great Indian bustards are endangered because of unrestricted hunting. The enormous bustard is often accompanied by other birds, like these bee-eaters. These eat the insects the bustard disturbs as it stalks the grasslands.

# Birds of prey

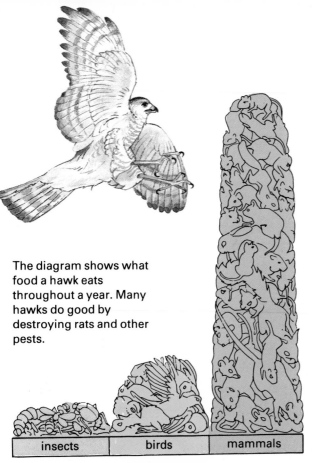

The diagram shows what food a hawk eats throughout a year. Many hawks do good by destroying rats and other pests.

| insects | birds | mammals |

Birds of prey are the most persecuted and misunderstood of all birds. Many are shot by farmers and hunters because they are suspected of killing livestock and game birds. Others are accidental victims of poison baits set out for wolves, coyotes and other predators. Some, like the magnificent peregrine falcon, have been seriously threatened as a result of eating birds contaminated by chemical pesticides sprayed over crops. Safer chemicals have now been developed, and the danger of poisoning is no longer such a threat.

Birds of prey suffer mostly because humans have given them a bad reputation, and wrongfully blamed them for many mishaps in the countryside. The larger eagles, for instance, readily feed on carrion, and can often be seen eating a farm animal such as a lamb. All too often, the farmer assumes

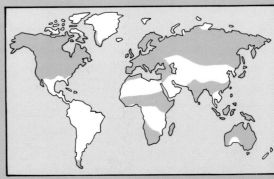

**The peregrine falcon**
The peregrine falcon is one of the most widely distributed birds (see map). They live by catching other birds on the wing. But they have become extremely rare wherever insecticides have been used. They were affected by the insecticides in the birds they ate, which built up in their bodies and made them unable to breed.

that the eagle is the killer, and shoots it. But although an eagle is capable of killing a lamb, it is far more likely that the animal was already dead or dying before the bird arrived on the scene.

Smaller birds of prey are blamed for killing game birds and chickens. Some varieties of falcon or hawk are occasionally guilty of this, but many other species rarely attack birds. Yet because all these birds look very similar to each other, the shooter does not distinguish between them, and they all suffer the same fate.

The amount of harm birds of prey do is vastly exaggerated, while their benefits to the farmer are not appreciated enough. They are particularly helpful because they kill an enormous number of rodents, which are the real pests to farms and crops.

Laws forbidding the killing of birds of prey are difficult to enforce, and many of these birds are becoming rare. The only way to make sure they stop being needlessly slaughtered is to educate people into realizing their true worth.

The golden eagle, like all eagles, has become very rare in settled areas. It has been poisoned or shot as a suspected threat to game or domestic animals. It has also suffered as its habitat has been invaded by people and the animals on which it preys have become scarce.

# Habitat destruction

The destruction of habitats is the single most important threat to bird life in the world today, and people are the main culprits.

As the human population grows, more land is taken over to meet our needs for food, homes, industry and commerce. So the natural vegetation and landscape which birds depend upon for their survival is destroyed. When this happens many birds starve, and some species, left without a place to live, become extinct.

This was the fate of the American ivory-billed woodpeckers. They lived in the ancient giant trees of the swamp forests, each bird needing about six square miles of unspoiled forest. Then all the big trees were cut for timber, and by the time people realized the predicament of the woodpecker, the damage had been done, and it was too late. The swamp forests took hundreds of years to grow and mature, and once they were cut down there was no way of replacing them in time for the birds to recover.

Marshland birds have also been seriously threatened. Many of the most spectacular species on earth are wetland dwellers. They include herons, storks, cranes, ibises, spoonbills and other smaller waders. These birds are endangered because their habitat is being taken over and transformed. Some marshlands are drained and converted into farmland. Some dry out when the underground water-level falls as water is pumped from wells. As the wetlands disappear, so the number of birds that live there diminishes as well.

Some birds can adapt to a changing environment, but they need a lot of time. In Europe, changes to the environment have

The large ivory-billed woodpecker has been a victim of the growth in our population. Left with nowhere to live, it is now believed to be extinct.

Kirtland's warbler only nests in burnt jack pines. Forestry management has reduced the number of fires, so land is now burned on purpose to give them a home.

been comparatively slow, taking thousands of years. The birds have had time to adjust, either by surviving in the wilder areas of woodland and country, or by gradually adapting to the changes. So, although some European birds have come under threat recently, not a single species has been lost so far.

In North America, however, enormous changes to the environment have occurred in just a few hundred years. Species such as the passenger pigeon and Carolina parakeet, have become extinct. Other birds there, including whooping cranes, trumpeter swans and snowy egrets, have been on the verge of extinction, and would not have survived but for the efforts of conservationists to provide sanctuaries for them.

The changes undergone by the developing countries during the present century have been even more rapid. Until recently, the tropical rain forests found in some of these countries were a paradise for birds. Nearly half of all the bird species in the world still live in the rain forests. But now the trees are being felled at a frightening rate. Unlike temperate forests, rain forests do not grow again if the land is abandoned after the trees have been cut down. The soil swiftly becomes infertile and bakes as hard as concrete. The land is then not only ruined for birds and animals, but is also useless to people because nothing will grow there. When the rain forests are destroyed they will be gone for ever, and many birds, animals and people will suffer as a result.

Kingfishers hunt by diving for fish. But pollution can cloud the water and kill the fish. Even if the fish survive the kingfisher cannot see to hunt.

# Sanctuary

Reserves for game birds have existed for a long time in countries all over the world. Their main purpose is to make sure that the birds survive in large numbers so that they can be shot for sport. But reserves simply to enable birds to live and breed in peace is a comparatively new idea.

North Americans have a proud record of establishing wildlife parks and guarding the birds and animals inside them. Americans are fortunate in having enough unspoiled land and sufficient money to make this possible. The setting-up of a reserve, which

has to be managed and policed, is an expensive project. Sometimes, routes of roads, and even railways, have had to be altered to avoid disturbing the larger reserves. This too is extremely costly.

In Africa, for instance, huge wildlife parks were established during colonial days. But now the African countries cannot spare enough money to maintain these reserves without help from richer western nations.

National and international organizations are helping to preserve the bird population by financing projects to protect birds and

**The Camargue**
The area bounded by the mouth of the River Rhone in France is a paradise for birds. It is just one example of an area which has been saved despite intense development around it. The panel shows just some of the birds which can be seen.

marsh harrier

hoopoe

little owl

bee-eater

roller

purple heron

little egret

spectacled warbler

avocet

night heron

black-winged stilt

penduline tit

provide them with sanctuaries all over the world. But money is not always the problem. Richer nations like Japan, and countries in Europe, are so densely populated and heavily industrialized that most of the land has been built on or cultivated. There is not enough room for big reserves. These countries have to make do with numerous small reserves.

In these crowded industrial countries the setting-up of reserves is often opposed by property-developers and commercial companies. When there is a shortage of space, people have strong views about how best to use it. Building houses and factories on the land would provide work and homes for a lot of people. So, from a commercial point of view, preserving land for the sake of a few wild birds might seem wasteful.

But it is also important to preserve as much of the natural environment as possible. After all, it is our responsibility to ensure that future generations will be able to enjoy the countryside and delight in the same beauty and variety of birds that can be seen today.

The Camargue is one of the last remaining homes in Europe of the greater flamingo.

# Rescue

If the population of a bird species drops seriously, great efforts are needed to save the bird from extinction. The success stories of the whooping crane and the trumpeter swan are examples of what can be done to save birds, if enough people care.

The whooping crane once lived on the swamps and prairies of North America, migrating southwards in the winter. As the American settlers worked their way westwards, they drained many of the swamps and hunted the birds. Egg and museum collectors reduced their numbers even further. But 1900 they were so rare that no young birds had been seen for thirty years.

In 1920, seventy-five cranes were counted as they wintered in the delta of the Gulf of Mexico, but by 1939 there were only fourteen survivors. The American government set up a huge project to save them. A refuge was established in Aransas county, Texas, and a massive publicity campaign was launched to prevent the birds being shot as they migrated. The decline was halted. Twenty-six whooping cranes were counted in 1940, and thirty-four in 1949.

Throughout this time no one knew where they bred. Then their last breeding ground was discovered in what was already a refuge – the Wood Buffalo Park in Canada. Eggs were taken to start captive breeding programs, and these have added to the security of the species. But although the whooping crane has made a remarkable recovery, there are still very few of them left in the wild.

The trumpeter swan also became endangered because its breeding grounds were invaded and it was overhunted. Once again, a huge rescue program was launched. Now there are at least 2,000 swans and they can be seen in several national parks in the western states of the USA.

Both the whooping crane and the trumpeter swan have the advantage of being large distinctive birds, easily recognizable and impressive enough to catch attention and public support. Unfortunately, some of the smaller and less appealing species can dwindle or die out with a dedicated few noticing their plight.

Trumpeter swans on migration. These birds are increasing in numbers now they have been given protection.

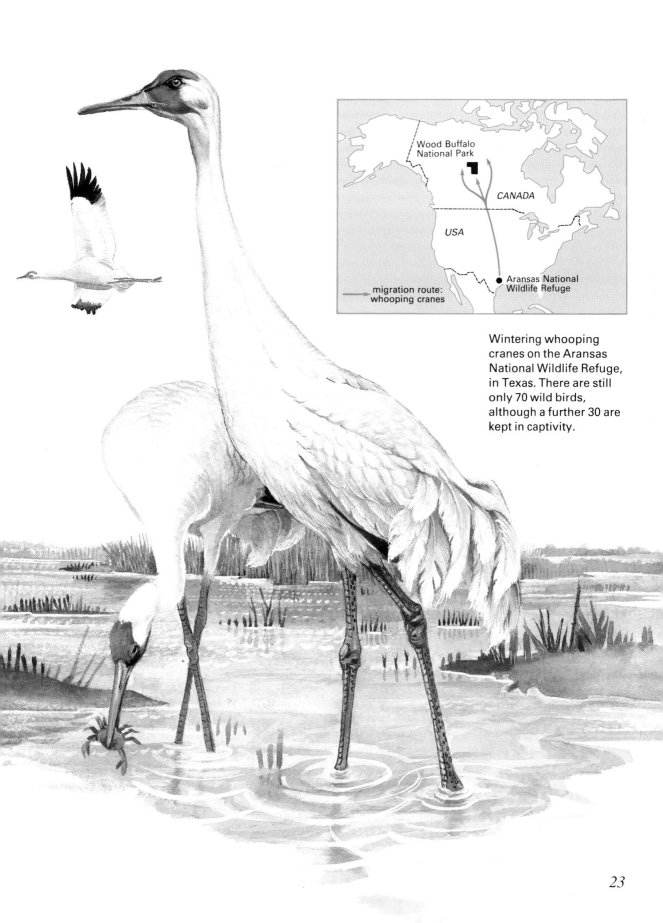

Wintering whooping cranes on the Aransas National Wildlife Refuge, in Texas. There are still only 70 wild birds, although a further 30 are kept in captivity.

Wood Buffalo National Park

CANADA

USA

Aransas National Wildlife Refuge

migration route: whooping cranes

# Captive breeding

When a species has dwindled to near extinction level, often the only hope of saving it is to try and breed birds in captivity. But captive breeding is not always successful, and there is the risk that very rare birds may be killed or injured during capture.

However, it is usually a risk worth taking, and the néné goose from Hawaii is a good example. There used to be about 25,000 of these in Hawaii, and in 1883 some were brought to Europe for collectors of ornamental water fowl. But by the 1940s, there were only fifty left in Hawaii, and it was extinct in Europe.

A captive breeding program was set up on the island. At the same time, two geese and a gander were sent to the Wildfowl Trust in Slimbridge, England. The gander became the ancestor of more than 250 birds, fifty of which were returned to the wild in Hawaii. Now the néné goose,

The néné goose and goslings. These birds have been saved by captive breeding.

**Birds in captivity**

Mikado pheasant

Swinhoe's pheasant

These are some of the spectacular pheasants which are extremely rare in the wild but are successfully bred in captivity.

Elliots pheasant

which is the national symbol of the island, is firmly established there.

The California condor is one of the world's rarest birds, and some are now being brought into captivity, in the hope that they may breed safely. However, not all birds of prey will breed in captivity. Many of them need to perform an aerial courtship display high in the sky before mating. This is impossible for caged birds. However, new methods, including artificial insemination, are now being developed to enable these captives to breed. But even so, the danger is that the fledglings will stay too tame to fend for themselves, because their parents cannot teach them to hunt for food in captivity. So they must be re-introduced into the wild very gradually.

It is always best for wild birds to live in freedom, but sadly some will only now survive as aviary birds because their natural habitat has been destroyed.

California condor

California condor in flight

These birds are beautiful in flight. Their wingspan is over 9.9 feet.

The California condor is very rare because it has been shot, and its habitat destroyed. Now it is hoped it can be saved by captive breeding.

# Home help

Helping birds is not just the responsibility of governments and large organizations. Each one of us can help in a small way.

Many threatened species live in countries far away, and although you can contribute to their welfare by joining one of the wildlife organizations, there is nothing you can do for them first-hand. But there are many ordinary birds on your own doorstep, and they need your help too.

The story of the American bluebird is a good example of the way in which families and individuals can contribute to bird survival. The bluebird is a favorite bird in America, like the robin is in Europe. Bluebirds were once a familiar sight in gardens along the eastern two-thirds of the United States. But then they became rare. The main reason for their decline was that they had nowhere to nest. These birds nest in the hollows of old trees. But old trees often become diseased or unsafe and have to be cut down. Many of them are felled simply to tidy up the landscape. In America, the disappearance of the old trees left the bluebirds without enough nesting sites.

People missed this popular bird, and many put nest boxes in their gardens, in the hope that the bluebirds would come back and thrive again. This went a long way towards saving them.

Then, with the organized setting-up of bluebird trails, which consisted of a series of nest boxes placed every 330 feet along a trail, bluebirds began to recover dramatically.

A nest box in your own garden will help many birds which live around you, including blue tits and great tits, and if you live in the country many of the more unusual birds like pied flycatchers will also be attracted. Choose the site of the nest box with care. Birds dislike damp or draughty places, and most prefer semi-shade where they are protected from too much fierce heat in the summer. The advantage of having a nest box is that you are not only helping the birds to breed and rear their young, but you also have the opportunity to study them at close hand in your own garden. Be careful not to disturb them, though, and never take the bird's eggs from the nest, even to hold them and look at them before putting them back. A mother bird will sometimes desert the nest if you do this. Many more birds will come into your garden if part of it can be left wild enough to provide cover for them, and if the use of poisonous insecticides is strictly limited.

Birds can be helped through a hard winter by feeding them and providing water

American bluebirds, like many other birds which nest in holes, welcome man-made nest-boxes.

in freezing weather. You can build a bird table, but be careful to place it safely out of the reach of neighboring cats. If the table is too near a fence, for instance, a cat can easily ambush the birds while they are busy feeding.

White bread is fine for birds, but soak it first and try to provide other foods, too. Many birds will welcome nuts, grain, butcher's suet, unroasted peanuts and meat bones. Avoid giving them rice because it swells in their stomachs.

If you find a fledgling which appears to have been deserted, it is best to leave it alone. Very often the parent bird is simply waiting for you to go away before reclaiming its young. If you come across an oiled seabird, don't try to help it yourself. Take it to the nearest ASPCA. Oiled birds can be saved with expert help, but it is a very specialized job.

Here are some young blue tits. Adult blue tits take advantage of nest boxes in parks or gardens, to breed and rear their young.

Feeding birds in winter can help many to survive. The birds shown here are all common visitors to European gardens.

greenfinch

European robin

song thrush

chaffinch

great tit

house sparrow

dunnock

# Saving the birds

Birds have to live more and more closely to humans as we take over a larger part of the world. To protect bird-life from harm, we must consider their needs and take care about what we are doing to the environment we share.

One major threat is pollution. Pollution is poison, caused by the smoke, waste matter, gases or chemicals, all of which are created by an industrial society. But it is not only birds which suffer. Air and water, plants, animals and humans can all suffer from the effects of pollution. It is in our own interests to reduce pollution in the world, and then of course the birds will benefit, too.

If you want to learn more about birds and take an active part in helping them, there are many ways of going about it. There are field study centers and bird observatories which run courses for young people. Or you can join one of the bird protection societies, or local nature clubs, which organize bird-watching outings and teaching programs.

The study of birds is called ornithology, and professional ornithology involves two main activities. Firstly, field work in which you go out and observe birds in their natural surroundings; and, secondly, scientific research and analysis in the laboratory and reference library. But anyone who is interested enough can study birds and perhaps even make important discoveries about them. Field work is one area in which amateurs can make a valuable contribution to scientific research, and add to our knowledge and understanding.

But the really important thing to remember is that you can do a lot to help birds just by caring about them and getting other people to care, too.

The densely populated
Netherlands is still the
home of these rare
spoonbills. They survive
because of the care and
concern of the people
there who make sure that
somewhere is still left for
them to live.

# Index

Illustrated by David Cook